Ernst Ludwig Kirchner

Edited By Lacey Belinda Smith

The Choice of Paris

Two Female Nudes At A Couch

Women

Two Nude Girls

Ernst Ludwig Kirchner (1880–1938) was a painter and printmaker born Aschaffenburg, Germany. He was a leading force behind the Expressionist movement in Germany. Kirchner was influenced by the work of Vincent van Gogh, Gustav Klimt, Edvard Munch, the Fauves, Japanese prints, African, and Oceanic art. He volunteered for army service in World War I, but soon he suffered a breakdown and was discharged from the army. The Nazis régime defamed his work as—degenerate--in 1937. They confiscated all of his paintings which were on display in public museums. In 1938 he committed suicide by a gunshot.

Two Girls 1907

Couple

1907—1908

Couples 1908

Nude Young Woman In Front Of A Oven—1905

Reclining Nude (Isabella)--1906

Bathing Women In A Room-- 1908

Macrella--1909

Lovers--1909

Milli--1909

Girl With Long Hair--1909

Small French--1909

Three Bathers On The Beach--1909

Crouching Girl--

1909

Dodo With Large Fan--Date: 1910

Female Artist--1910

Girl With Cat (Franzi)--1910

Hamburg Dancers

1910

Playing People--1910

Half-Naked Woman With A Hat--1911

Female Nude Kneeling Before A Red Screen--1912

English Dance Couple

Woman Before The Mirror--
1912

Two Bathers--

1912

Female Nudes Striding Into The Sea--

1912

Stooping Act In Space--

1912

Nude Woman Combing Her Hair--

1913

Three Bathers--1913

Bathers On The Lawn--1914

Two Yellow Knots With Bunch Of Flowers--1914

Bathers at Sea--1914

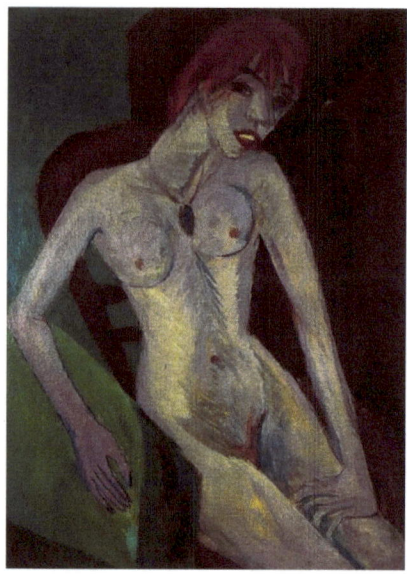

Capelli Rossi (Red Hair)--
1914

After the Bath –1914

The Tent--1914

Dance School--1914

The Dance Between The Women--
1915

Man And Naked Woman--
1915

Self Portrait as a Soldier - Ernst Ludwig Kirchner--1915

Two Nudes In The Wood II--1926

Naked Girl Behind The Curtain (Franzi)
1910—1926

Three Nudes In The Forest—1928

Naked Women On Meadow--
1928

Entcounter--1929

Nude In Orange And Yellow
1929--1930

Nudes In A Meadow--
1929

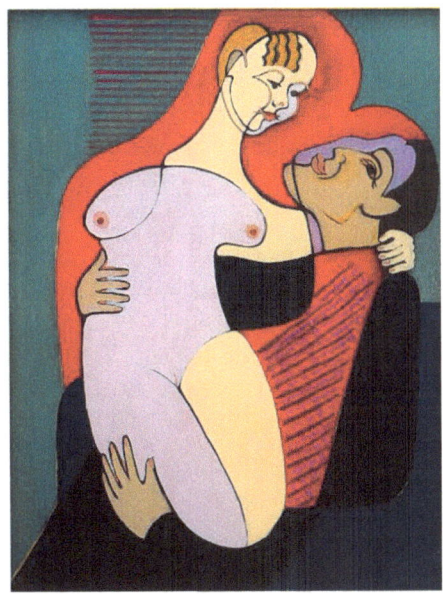

Great Lovers (Mr And Miss Hembus)

1930--Cubism

Reclining Nude In A Bathtub With Pulled On Legs--1930

Reclining Female Nude—1931

Artist And Female Model--1933

Colourful Dance--

1933

Couple In A Room

Dance Of Negros

Blond Woman In A Red Dress, Portrait Of Elisabeth Hembus--1932

Bathing Women Between White Rocks

Colourful Dance

Women Playing With A Ball
1931-1932

Lovers (The Kiss)—1930-- Cubism

Three Nudes And Reclining Man--

1934

Bathers On The Lawn

Portrait Of Art Dealer Manfred Shames

1925-1932

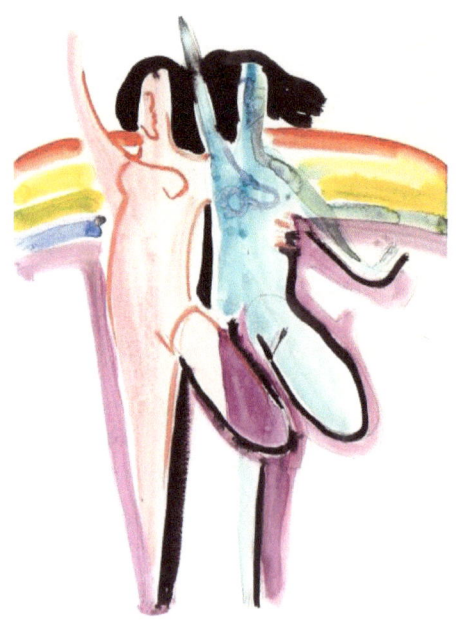

Design For The Banquet Hall In Essen

1932-1933

Female Nude with Black Hat

Five Bathing Women At A Lake

Japanese Parasol

Female Dancer 1933

Standing Female Nude In Front Of A Tent

Practising Dancer
1934

Arching Girls In The Wood--1934

www.ingramcontent.com/pod-product-compliance
Lightning Source LLC
Chambersburg PA
CBHW050404180526
45159CB00005B/2148